Information Systems Engineering Library

PCTE – An Overview

Karen Thompson

CCTA

November 1993

LONDON: HMSO

© Crown Copyright 1993

Applications for reproduction should be made to HMSO

First published 1993

ISBN 0 11 330595 8

For further information regarding this publication and other CCTA products please contact:

CCTA Library
Riverwalk House
157-161 Millbank
London SW7P 4RT

071-217-3331

Contents

Foreword

Acknowledgements

1 Introduction   1

    1.1   Purpose of this volume
    1.2   Who should read this volume
    1.3   Structure of the volume
    1.4   Related reading

2 The place of PCTE in ISE   3

    2.1   IS provision policies
    2.2   Information Systems Engineering
    2.3   Environments
    2.4   PCTE

3 Open integrated development environments   13

    3.1   Why use an environment?
    3.2   Services needed in an environment
    3.3   Openness
    3.4   Integration
    3.5   How an open integrated development environment is built up

4 The PCTE standard   29

    4.1   What the PCTE standard addresses
    4.2   Areas that the PCTE standard does not address
    4.3   Evolution of the PCTE standard
    4.4   Form of the PCTE standard
    4.5   Commercial and government acceptance
    4.6   Conformance with the PCTE standard
    4.7   PCTE and other standards

5 The PCTE open repository   39

    5.1   The structure of the repository
    5.2   Data models
    5.3   Data protection and security

6 PCTE environments and tools   47

  6.1 What is a PCTE environment?
  6.2 Services provided by PCTE environments
  6.3 Openness of PCTE environments
  6.4 Integration in PCTE environments

7 Choosing a PCTE based development environment   59

  7.1 Aims of defining IS provision policies
  7.2 When an application development environment is appropriate
  7.3 The role of PCTE
  7.4 Procurement considerations
  7.5 Costs and benefits

Annex   67

  A   Data modelling in PCTE

Bibliography   73

Glossary   77

Index   81

Foreword

The **Information Systems Engineering Library** provides guidance on managing and carrying out Information Systems Engineering activities. In the IS life cycle, Information Systems Engineering takes place once the IS strategy has been defined. It is concerned with the development and ongoing improvement of information systems up to the operational stage, when systems become the responsibility of infrastructure management.

The Information Systems Engineering Library builds on guidance in the CCTA IS Guides, particularly set A: *Management and Planning Set* and set B: *Systems Development Set* and complements other CCTA products, in particular the project management method, PRINCE, and the systems analysis and design method, SSADM.

Volumes in the Information Systems Engineering Library are of interest to varying levels of staff from IS directors to IS providers, helping them to improve the quality and productivity of their IS development work. Some volumes in this library should also be of interest to business managers, IS users and those involved in market testing, whose business operations depend on having effective IS support by means of Information Systems Engineering activities.

The Information Systems Engineering Library also complements other related CCTA publications, particularly the IT Infrastructure Library for operational issues and the IS Planning Subject Guides for strategic issues.

CCTA welcomes customer views on Information Systems Engineering Library publications. Please send your comments to:

Customer Services
Information Systems Engineering Group
Gildengate House
Upper Green Lane
NORWICH
NR3 1DW

Acknowledgements

The main body of the volume was prepared for the CCTA by Margaret Aldis of Syntagma. It was reviewed for technical aspects of PCTE by Jonathan Jowett and Ian Campbell of GIE Emeraude, who provided a number of helpful comments.

Chapter 1
Introduction

1 Introduction

1.1 Purpose of this volume

The purpose of this volume is to explain how the Portable Common Tool Environment (PCTE) standard may be of relevance to organisational policies for information systems development — often referred to as Information Systems Engineering (ISE).

PCTE is an interface standard which defines an open repository and specifies a set of facilities on which CASE (Computer Aided Systems Engineering) tools, and other services, can be built. Its aim is to support the development of open and integrated environments for systems engineering projects. This volume provides an overview of the purpose and technical features of the PCTE standard, and of application development environments and CASE tools built upon it. It shows how the PCTE standard helps provide important characteristics that are needed in application development environments and tools. It also summarises some procurement considerations when choosing PCTE tools and environments.

The volume outlines the background to the development of the standard and its future. It provides references to where more detailed information can be obtained. The relationship of PCTE to other standards is also described.

1.2 Who should read this volume

This volume is aimed at the following readers:

- those responsible for defining an organisation's information systems technical policies that are concerned with the way information systems are to be designed, developed and maintained

- those responsible for specifying and delivering the organisation's information systems, whether these are developed in-house or procured from external suppliers

- those responsible for specifying and procuring ISE services for the organisation's businesses

- those responsible for specifying and procuring CASE tools and for Application Development Environment support to an organisation's Information Systems Engineering activities

- those responsible for planning and monitoring the overall investment an organisation has in information systems and ISE services.

1.3 **Structure of the volume**

Chapter 2 explains the relevance of PCTE to Information Systems Engineering and introduces the issues addressed in the volume. Chapter 3 provides an overview of the kind of ISE environment that is needed by organisations, and the benefits seen by both IS customers and IS providers.

Chapters 4 to 6 describe various aspects of PCTE in more detail, showing how they meet the requirements discussed in Chapter 3. Chapter 4 defines the scope of the PCTE standard, its acceptance and commercial availability, and its relationship to other standards in this area. Chapter 5 describes the PCTE repository, and Chapter 6 PCTE environments and tools.

Finally, Chapter 7 provides a summary of the key factors to be considered in choosing a development environment based on the PCTE standard within a policy for ISE provision.

1.4. **Related reading**

This volume is intended to provide an overview of the PCTE standards and how they may be of relevance to organisations. Further detailed guidance on PCTE can be found in the Prentice Hall publication of *PCTE the standard for open repositories*. Publication details can be found in the bibliography section.

2 The place of PCTE in ISE

PCTE is an international and widely accepted standard that has been developed as part of the computer industry's response to the problems of systems development. It is expected to be one of the foundations of new levels of support for the provision of information systems, which will bring benefits to both providers and users of those systems.

This chapter gives an overview of what PCTE means to those involved in the planning, specification, development and use of information systems, whether they are produced in-house or obtained from external suppliers.

2.1 IS provision policies

An organisations's IS provision policies define how the organisation specifies and obtains the information systems and services it requires. The level at which the system development process, methods and ISE services need to be defined depends on whether the information systems are to be developed in-house, contracted-out, or bought-in as off-the-shelf products.

In-house development

If the organisation develops its own information systems, it will own both the information systems themselves and any tools or other supporting systems used in their development. This means that policies must ensure that the ISE environment within the organisation offers value for money, ease of use and flexibility, as well as delivering information systems that meet the needs of the organisation.

Contracted-out development

If the information systems are developed by external suppliers, under contract, the organisation will not be directly concerned with costs or ease of use of ISE services, except in so far as they affect the costs and timescales of contractors' tenders. Nevertheless, the organisation may still wish to specify aspects of the system development process for a number of reasons.

The organisation will want its information systems to be developed in a way that ensures their quality and timeliness, and will need to avoid becoming dependent on a single IS provider.

By defining ISE policies that allow deliverables to be moved freely during the system development process, the organisation can increase the possibilities of competitive tendering. For example, the organisation may invite tenders for fixed-term contracts, or for design, software development and maintenance as separate stages. In the event of failure to deliver or other supplier difficulties, the organisation can preserve its investment in work-in-progress, rather than being tied to the software and hardware suppliers selected at the start of the development project.

Off-the-shelf systems

If the organisation's IS needs are to be met by procuring off-the-shelf products, it may wish to give preference to those that are developed and maintained using respected methods, as some assurance of quality, value for money, and continued maintenance even in the event of the original developer abandoning the product. This might extend to specification of availability of source code in particular languages, or to design specifications defined in terms of particular formal methods (SSADM, say). It is unlikely to extend to a need to specify the ISE system used.

2.2 Information Systems Engineering

The need to view information systems development as an engineering discipline has arisen from the ever increasing demand for software of all types. In particular, attention has focused on the difficulties experienced with the development of large, complex and mission-critical systems, and the benefits to be gained with improved methods and control.

Chapter 2
The place of PCTE in ISE

As hardware costs have fallen, and power increased, the number and complexity of potential applications have increased. The costs of software development and maintenance have come to represent an increasingly large proportion of system costs. Moreover, with the growing dependence on software in every sphere of activity — from finance to aerospace, from health care to decision support — it becomes more and more vital to have assured reliability and timeliness of delivery and well as flexibility and ease of modification.

Over the past ten years or so, a good deal of common understanding has developed about how to make systems development more efficient and predictable. There has been a convergence of ideas coming from academic research, from major systems users, and from computer manufacturers and software suppliers. These ideas draw not only on systems development experience but also on work in information management, analogies with other engineering areas and quality management standards. Three general lines of approach are agreed to be particularly relevant.

Process models

Systems development should follow a defined *process*, covering design, development, testing, delivery and support. A number of different lifecycle models have been proposed, and although these differ in detail they all allow the process to be broken down into separate phases, within which tasks and responsibilities can be clearly defined. This in turn allows project management methods such as PRINCE to be applied, and quality management systems to be defined.

Methods and techniques

Methods address the problems of particular systems development activities. They formalise the description of various aspects of the system under development, and allow the use of effective techniques. An example is the Structured Systems Analysis and Design Method (SSADM) which enables systems designers to make a systematic breakdown of requirements to arrive at a set of functions that can be implemented.

PCTE - An Overview

CASE tools

The third line of approach is 'computer aiding' the systems development process. A large number of CASE tools have been developed. Some support particular phases of the lifecycle and, especially, particular techniques and methods; others support general activities such as project management and document processing. The first group of tools are often referred to as 'lifecycle tools' or 'vertical tools'. The second group are referred to as 'cross lifecycle tools' or 'horizontal tools'.

This is illustrated in Figure 1 which shows a partial view of a systems development lifecycle.

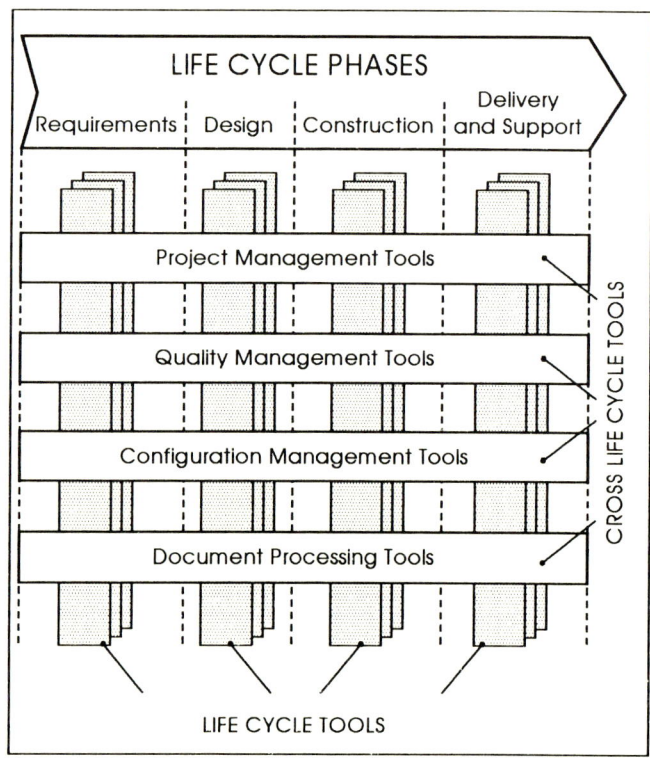

Figure 1: CASE tools in a systems development lifecycle

Chapter 2
The place of PCTE in ISE

The improvements in efficiency and accuracy achieved by using CASE tools for individual activities have led to over-expectations and resulting disappointments. It is now generally recognised that automating parts of the development process cannot by itself improve the control and efficiency of the whole. The real problem to solve is how to control and share the information and the products that the CASE tools work on, so that the complex relationships between, for example, the design, the code written to meet the design, the allocation of the project team, and the delivered system, are maintained and utilised through the entire lifecycle. Failure to tackle this problem leads to duplication and incompatibility of information. For example, if minor changes in program structure introduced during coding cannot be automatically fed back to the design tool, the formal design specification may well be left inaccurate, and its potential for use in later stages of the lifecycle such as delivery and maintenance, or for reuse in future developments, will be compromised.

2.3 Environments

The aim of providing support for ISE throughout the lifecycle has led to the concept of a complete *Systems Engineering Environment* or *Application Development Environment* as illustrated in Figure 2. This is a computer system whose purpose is to support systems development. It is distinct from the applications that are developed within it, and may well be a physically separate system, running on a different type of hardware.

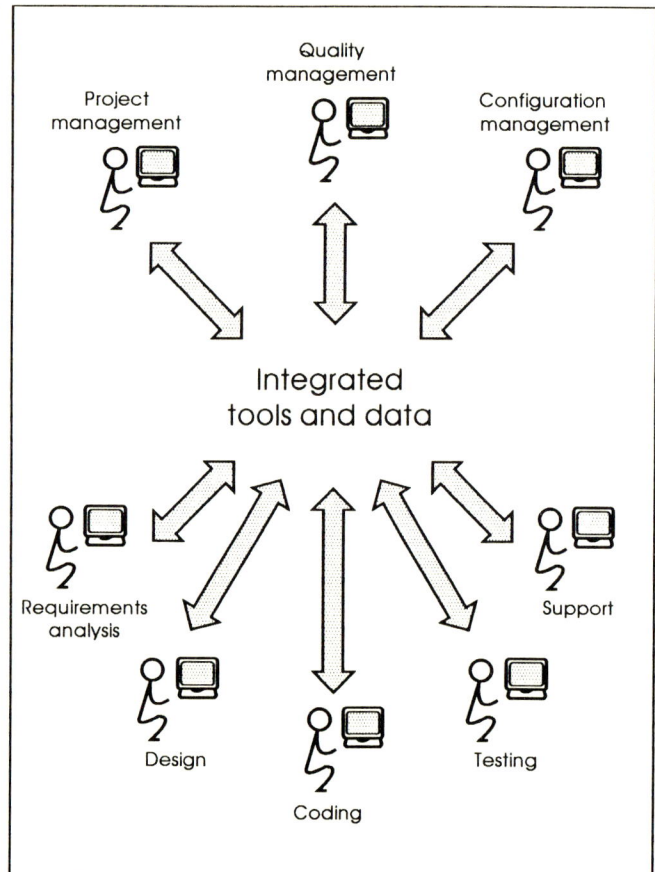

Figure 2: An integrated application development environment

In order to meet the need to share and control project and product data, and to allow individual CASE tools to work together within a defined process, an application development environment needs to be *integrated*.

In order to avoid proprietary lock-in, so that information systems can be developed and maintained over time without the IS customer becoming tied to a single environment supplier or IS provider, environments need to be *open*. These two characteristics, and the benefits they offer to systems developers and to the users of the information systems they produce, are discussed in detail in Chapter 3.

They can be summarised as follows:

- Integration. The environment should offer seamless support for the systems development process. This means that tools should interwork, sharing data as appropriate, and interacting with tool users in similar ways. A key element in integration is the existence of an integrated database or *repository* to hold all the products and information associated with the systems development projects. This allows data to be shared between CASE tools, and avoids redundancy and inconsistency in the data. It also allows users of the environment to consult the data directly using database management tools

- Openness. It should be possible for the environment to run on a variety of different manufacturers' equipment, and to incorporate tools from different sources. It should be possible to move tools and data from one environment to another.

In the past, high levels of integration have only been achievable at the expense of openness. This conflict must be addressed by basing the environment on widely accepted, non-proprietary, standards. This is the frame of reference of the PCTE standard.

2.4 PCTE

PCTE is an interface standard which defines an open repository and specifies a set of facilities on which CASE tools, and the other services of the environment, can be built. Its aim is to support the development of integrated and open environments. The standard itself, therefore, is not one that applies to the developed information systems, but to the ISE tools and environments that may be used during systems development.

The importance of PCTE to readers of this volume lies in the characteristics it implies and instils in the tools and environments which make use of the standard interfaces, and in the resulting benefits seen in systems developed with their support. Any examination of the relevance of PCTE to defining and meeting technical policies for ISE, therefore, requires an understanding of what PCTE means in the following contexts:

- The PCTE standard. In choosing to commit to any standard, it is important to have a clear understanding of the issues the standard seeks to address, the likely evolution and take-up, and the relationship to other standards. Chapter 4 addresses these issues

- The PCTE repository. The PCTE repository is at the heart of any PCTE environment and is the principal mechanism for ensuring integration and openness. Chapter 5 gives an overview of the key concepts of the repository

- PCTE environments. These are environments which are built on the PCTE interfaces and include a PCTE repository. A commitment to PCTE is a commitment to use a PCTE environment for systems development, either within the organisation or as a criterion for external IS providers. The features and availability of PCTE environments, and the considerations of choice of environment, are discussed in Chapter 6

- PCTE tools. One of the main benefits of a policy based on PCTE is the freedom to choose tools individually because they support a particular method or offer the best value for money. Chapter 6 covers aspects to be considered in choosing tools, what constitutes a PCTE tool and how other tools may be integrated into a PCTE environment.

Figure 3 illustrates the relationship between these concepts.

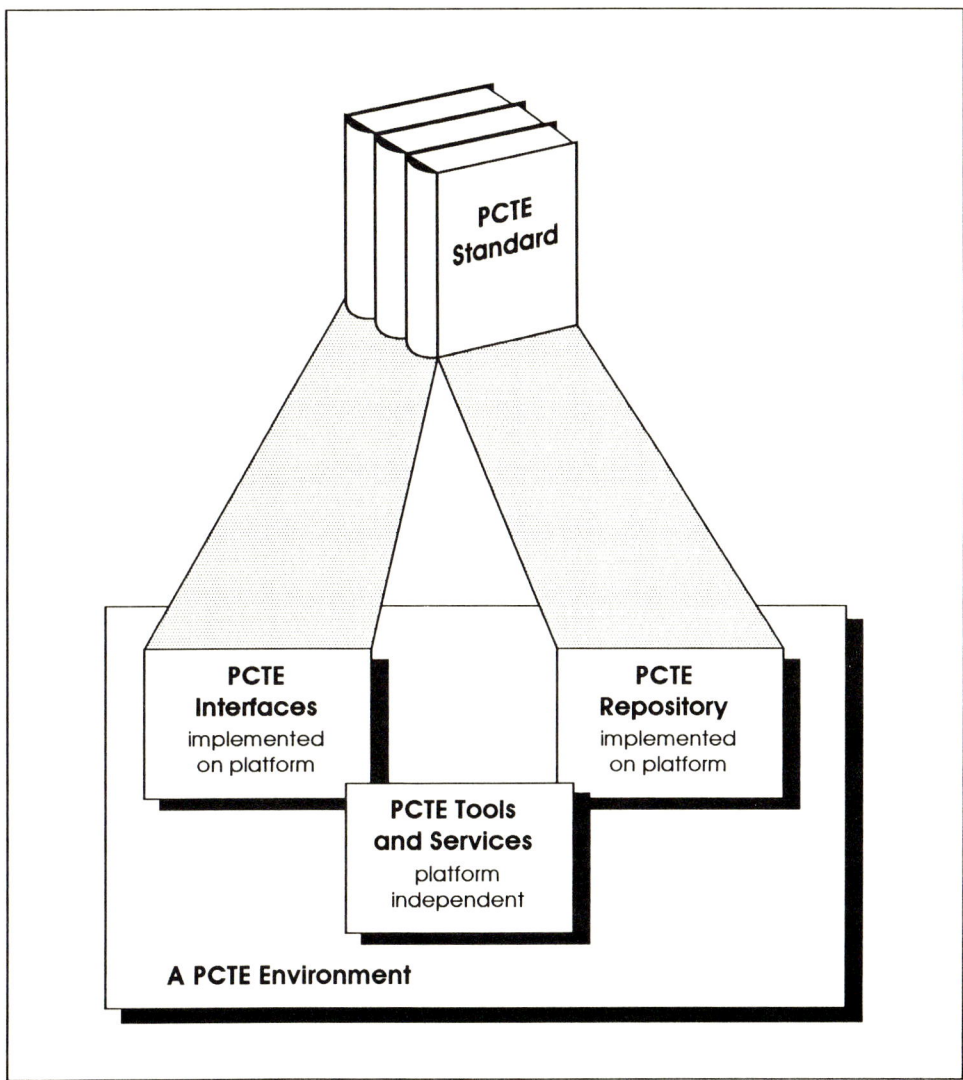

Figure 3: Scope of the PCTE standard

3 Open integrated development environments

This chapter defines the key characteristics of an open integrated development environment. It shows how these characteristics can help ensure that an organisation's needs are fully met by the information systems developed within such an environment. It also provides the background against which the details of PCTE given in Chapters 4 to 6 can be evaluated.

3.1 Why use an environment?

When a new information system is to be developed, whether in-house or contracted-out, there are a number of basic needs that must be met. First and foremost, the delivered system must satisfy quality requirements, in terms of 'fitness for purpose'. In other words, it must be correctly specified and it must meet the specification. The delivered system must be produced on time and represent good value for money.

Flexibility is also important. The developed systems may be required to run on other hardware, or to be upgraded or changed over time. Having made an investment in the development of one system, the organisation may want to reuse components of the system, such as software modules, documentation, specifications and designs, in other developments. Last but not least, the organisation will want to avoid proprietary lock-in, not only in the developed systems, but in their method of production. Where systems are to be produced within the organisation, the organisation must not be locked into a particular tool or environment supplier. Where they are to be contracted-out it is even more important to ensure that systems development and maintenance are not locked into a single IS provider, tool or method.

Quality management, control over development schedules, and flexibility all depend on establishing a well defined systems development and maintenance process, and on making use of suitable methods and tools. As discussed in Chapter 2, current thinking suggests that the best support for systems development will come from using application development environments that are both open and integrated. The aim is to provide full project support to the IS provider and thus promote efficient, controlled systems development, while avoiding dependence on any particular supplier. This in turn means that the environments must make it easy to integrate hardware, supporting software, tools and services from different suppliers, and for these suppliers to create high quality, good value products.

The benefits to be gained from using an open integrated development environment are greatest where:

- the information systems are complex

- the information systems are safety-critical

- the development team is large

- the development is to be split amongst different IS providers

- the information systems need to be maintained over long periods of time

- the products of the development process (software, designs, documentation) may need to be reused elsewhere

- details of the system development project history need to be formally maintained.

Chapter 3
Open integrated development environments

Conversely, information systems requirements that are simple and immediate may be satisfied more cheaply and easily by using market-proven packaged products, or by developing ad-hoc in-house programs, accepting that such systems may have limited flexibility and life.

It is important to realise that the use of an open integrated environment will not of itself ensure that the organisation's ISE needs will be met. In order to make good use of the potential of such an environment, without simply adding cost and effort overheads to no effect, the organisation must have a well defined lifecycle and quality management system, and management and staff on the project must be able and willing to comply with, and make use of, these. This situation is often described as 'process maturity', and is discussed by Watts Humphrey in *Managing the Software Process*.

3.2 Services needed in an environment

The first demand on the application development environment is that it should provide all the *services* needed to support the systems development process: the development activities, the control of development projects, and the administration of the environment itself. In this context, services may be tools or supporting functions. They may therefore support the environment user directly, as when a project manager uses a data query tool, for instance, or indirectly, when the tools or functions are used by other tools.

The listing and classification of the types of services that might be needed in an environment are the subject of several initiatives by governments and standards bodies. A number of 'reference models' or 'taxonomies' have been developed and may be used as a basis for evaluating and comparing environments. Different development environments will contain different ranges of services, depending on the types of products and processes being supported. The way in which specific environments can be built up is discussed further in section 3.5. The availability of services in PCTE environments is addressed in Chapter 6.

The following sections give some examples of the kinds of services that may be needed in an environment.

Specification and design services

These are tools, sometimes known as 'front-end' or 'upper' CASE tools, which support techniques for systems analysis, requirements specification, and program and data design. The tools needed will depend on the methods used by the organisation, such as CRAMM for risk analysis and SSADM for systems analysis and design.

Software development services

These are so called 'back-end' or 'lower' CASE tools, which support the development of the software itself. They may include syntax-directed editors, compilers, debugging tools and so on. The choice of tools in this area depends on the programming languages and coding standards to be used, and on the target hardware for the developed systems. Since the application may well be intended to run on hardware different to that of the environment itself, and since there may be more than one target, the environment may need to include cross-compilers and/or some method of down loading code to the target system.

Version and configuration management services

Many items produced during systems development (specifications, plans, code, documentation) exist in more than one version, and the environment should include facilities to support the management and control of these versions. The environment should also provide configuration management facilities, which allow the correct versions of a number of components to be gathered together when, for example, a product is delivered.

Project control services	The environment needs to offer traditional project management tools such as estimation, time and resource scheduling, and time recording tools. It may also need to include other services related to project control, such as tools to monitor and control work flow, and services to support change management. Once again, the services needed by any particular organisation will depend on the methods and standards it wishes to use.
User communication services	If the environment is to be used by all the staff working on a project, it needs to provide services to support CSCW (Computer Supported Cooperative Work). These may include services to support group working, action reporting and decision making, as well as more traditional services such as electronic mail and notice boards.
Documentation management and publishing services	Application development projects need to produce many different types of document. These include management documentation (such as proposals, procedures and standards), documentation produced as part of the systems development process (such as specifications), and user documentation to be delivered as part of the application itself. These documents need to be managed as data items, and printed or delivered electronically in appropriate formats.
Data management and query services	The environment must include services to manage the many different types of data used in the environment. Services are needed for data modelling, management of a shared data repository, and access to the data by environment users and tools. Data management services have to ensure that data consistency, privacy and integrity are maintained, and that there is resilience to failures, even when the data is being accessed by many different users and tools, and when it may be distributed over a network.

	System administration	Like a conventional operating system, the environment services has to provide system administration facilities. This includes management of the physical environment, setting up and managing the users and resources of the environment, taking back-ups, and similar activities.
3.3	**Openness**	An open environment is one which can include hardware and software from a variety of independent suppliers. This implies:

- the ability to run on a range of hardware and operating systems

- the ability to incorporate tools from different sources

- the ability to transfer data between tools and between environments.

3.3.1 The benefits of openness

Openness is important for a number of reasons. Any application development environment represents a considerable investment in hardware and software, and will quickly contain a wealth of valuable data, reusable products and so on. It is therefore extremely desirable, whether the environment is provided in-house or belongs to an outside IS provider, that it is not tied to one manufacturer's or supplier's equipment or software, and that the data used by tools in one environment can be understood in another. Openness allows IS providers to change environment without losing valuable information and tools. It frees IS customers to change IS provider, or to use several IS providers working on different parts of the system or its lifecycle.

Many CASE tools are complex and highly specialised, and the ideal choices are likely to be market leaders, produced by different specialist suppliers. Openness makes it possible to create environments which contain the most suitable tools, chosen for their quality, value for money and applicability to particular methods and techniques. It should be possible to build an environment that brings together the chosen tools, from whatever source. The environment should be open to the addition of new tools as required to support changes in systems development processes, or to replace a tool with a better one to do the same job.

3.3.2 The need for standards

Proprietary environments can offer a degree of openness. For instance, they may allow third party tools to be integrated and they may run on a range of hardware. True openness, however, needs to be based on established standards.

On the one hand, there are *de facto* standards, which originate in proprietary or research developments but which, either because of their intrinsic merit or the status of the original supplier, become very widely used by many different suppliers. De facto standards can offer considerable openness, but since there is no regulatory body it is possible that incompatible variants or competitors will appear.
De jure or formal standards, on the other hand, are developed and reviewed by experts drawn from a range of commercial and academic backgrounds, and specifically address the problems of evolution and conformance.

Software from different sources conforming to the same standard should achieve the highest degree of interworking. However, it is important, in basing a policy on de jure standards, to make sure the standards are likely to be widely implemented. Commitment to a standard which is then not widely taken up could still leave an organisation locked into the only commercial implementation, for instance.

There are two key areas where standards are needed to ensure openness: tool interfaces and tool data models. Both these areas are addressed by the PCTE standard, as discussed in Chapter 4.

Tool interfaces

Tool interfaces are the functions used by the tool to interface with the user, with other tools, and with the resources of the environment, including data handling. The use of proprietary, low level interfaces such as file handling routines offered by an operating system, or screen handling commands related to particular hardware, leaves the tool tied to those systems.

The need is for a defined set of *Public Tool Interfaces* (PTI) implemented on many different proprietary systems. Tools can then run on different platforms simply by recompiling the tool source code with appropriate libraries. A standardised and generally accepted PTI is an advantage to tool suppliers in that it provides a larger, more stable market than individual proprietary systems can offer. It makes it more possible for tool developers to invest in high quality tools, and means that the development effort can be concentrated on the tool rather than on porting it to many different platforms. This in turn gives the IS provider, and indirectly the IS customer, the advantage of high quality tools at the best possible price.

Tool data models

Tool data models need to be standardised at two levels. Firstly, there need to be standard ways of defining the models, so that the models can be commonly understood. These ways of defining models are sometimes referred to as 'metamodels', by analogy with the use of 'metalanguages' to define the syntax of computer programming languages. Secondly, the data models themselves need to be standardised so that, for example, all tools which handle a 'task' or a 'user' or a 'C language source file' agree on the meaning of these data items.

3.4 Integration

3.4.1 The benefits of integration

For an environment to offer complete support and control for systems development, the services it provides should be integrated. Integration gives added value to the environment components — when tools and data are integrated, the whole is greater than the sum of the parts. To take a simple example, in an integrated environment a query tool can be used on the results produced by a project management tool to obtain ad hoc information on the state of the project. Integration also allows higher levels of support and control. For example, because all tasks are carried out within the environment, and all results stored within it, progress can be directly monitored by an integrated work flow service, rather than being indirectly (and perhaps inaccurately) reported on.

Individual components can be simpler and can avoid duplicating facilities when they are to be used in an integrated environment. For instance, many tools need to offer basic text editing to allow users to input data, but if they can all make use of the same text editing service there is no need for these facilities to be recreated in each tool.

Finally, integration reduces complexity for staff working on systems development. They can work within a single environment, without having to learn different tool interfaces or manually transfer information from one tool to another.

Integration thus offers the possibility of providing better support more simply and at less cost, and of improving the quality and reusability of the developed information systems.

3.4.2 The three axes of integration

The extent to which environments may be integrated is often analyzed against three independent axes.

These axes, which are shown in Figure 4, are defined in the following way.

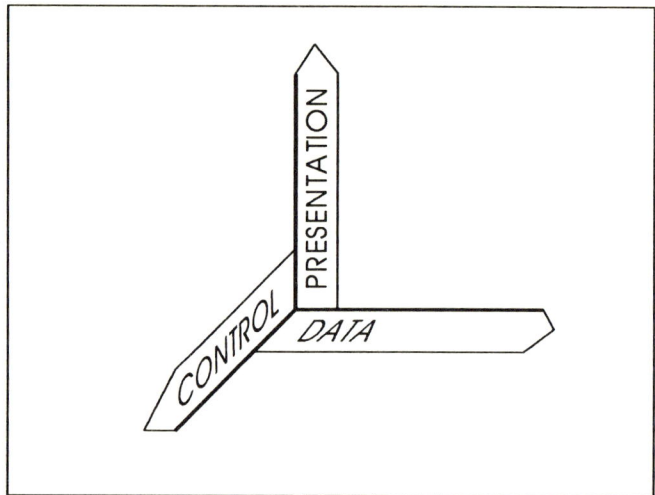

Figure 4: The three integration axes

Data integration

Data integration is concerned with making the data used by tools 'public' rather than locked into specific tools, and thus allowing it to be shared within and between environments. This gives the data handled by tools added value, and in particular makes the systems engineering products held in the environment (code modules, designs, documents) reusable. File-based systems generally offer only low levels of data integration, since potentially shareable items of data may be locked within a tool-specific file format. High levels of data integration can be achieved with a fully open repository based on common data models.

Chapter 3
Open integrated development environments

Control integration — Control integration covers the degree to which services work cooperatively. There are two aspects to this. Firstly, it covers communication, in the sense that services may call other services or exchange messages while they are running. An environment which is well integrated in this respect can be built up from smaller, more modular services, rather than from monolithic tools that duplicate functions found elsewhere.

The second aspect of control integration is integration of tool use within a process. A highly integrated environment in this sense would be one where the work flow of the project automatically makes tools available or performs certain functions at appropriate times.

Presentation integration — Presentation integration is about giving a common 'look and feel' to the user interface of the environment. The representation of the different types of data in the environment, the ways in which the user uses keyboard and mouse, initiates operations, obtains Help and so on should be common across all the tools of the environment. This makes tools easier to use efficiently and accurately, and thus helps IS providers to develop applications quickly, cheaply and well.

Low levels of presentation integration are achieved by asking that all tools conform to certain standards, as set out in a 'Style Guide', for instance. At higher levels of integration, the environment supports and enforces the common look and feel by providing presentation services to handle tools' user interface requirements. Such services are often referred to as UIMSs (User Interface Management Services).

3.5 How an open integrated development environment is built up

3.5.1 Layered architecture

Although open integrated development environments could take different physical forms and architecture, the concepts are best understood as a layered architecture as illustrated in Figure 5.

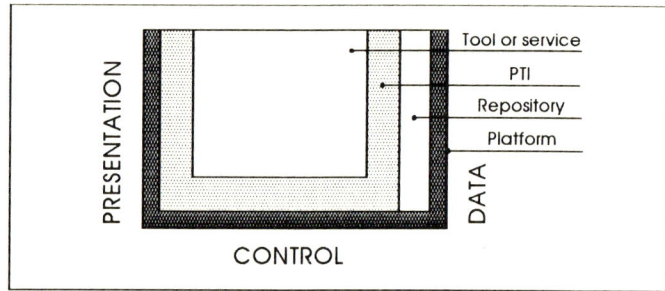

Figure 5: Layering in an open integrated environment

Platform

In Figure 5, the outer layer represents the hardware and related software of the platform. This may be an 'open platform', conforming to the ISO POSIX standards (see section 4.7), or it may be an operating system or Database Management System (DBMS). The platform provides its own mechanisms to handle data access, program execution and control, and the user interface.

The ideal type of hardware for an environment designed to support large development projects provides each user with a high-performance workstation with a graphical user interface. These workstations are connected on a network, with associated resources such as printers, data storage and back-up facilities. Using a network has the advantage that users can share software and physical resources.

Chapter 3
Open integrated development environments

Environments based on mainframes or minicomputers are also possible. However, they are more prone to overloading if, for example, several team members simultaneously wish to compile, perform critical path analyses, or run other tools needing a lot of processing power. Stand-alone systems, while potentially offering good development environments for single users, cannot offer a fully integrated project support environment, which implies the use of a shared repository by team members. Working with separate databases inevitably means that there will be fragmentation, duplication and inconsistencies in the data.

Repository

The repository is implemented on the platform, making use of the storage facilities and data access mechanisms that the platform provides. In a distributed architecture, the repository has to be accessible from all workstations. It could be held as a central resource (a database server), or it could be distributed over the storage devices of the network. The latter approach is likely to give more resilience to failure and faster access times, but requires more powerful data management facilities.

Tool interfaces

The next layer represents the Public Tool Interfaces. Tools and services built on this layer have access to the repository and resources of the environment without any dependence on the underlying platform.

Layering may also be used at higher levels, to make commonly used functions available to all tools in the environment. These higher level interfaces are sometimes referred to as 'common services'. They are of particular significance in supporting integration within a specific environment. While the PTI must by definition be applicable across a wide range of environments, whatever type of user and systems development they are to support, these higher level services can address more specific needs.

For example, an environment might offer basic editing facilities as a common service, which would ensure these facilities were provided in a standard way in all tools that used the service. Another example would be a user interface management service (UIMS) to provide standard user interface facilities.

3.5.2 Environment building

Creating an environment from component parts, some of which will have been purchased separately from independent suppliers, is referred to as *environment building*. This is best understood as a two-stage process in which the *framework* is distinct from the full environment.

The framework provides the PTI, repository, and all the software and data needed to support integration and provide general purpose services. It may include cross lifecycle tools and tools for environment administration, as well as libraries of tool interfaces. ECMA and NIST have jointly developed a reference model to define what services may be needed in such frameworks. The model is often illustrated by the so-called 'toaster diagram', shown in Figure 6. This diagram does not show the full extent of the reference model, and it should not be interpreted literally as a system architecture. It is not an illustration of PCTE. It does however give some feeling for the way in which the full environment is built up from selected tools which can be 'slotted into' a framework of services supporting presentation, data and control aspects of integration.

Although a framework may itself be composed of software from different sources, one would expect it to appear as a separate product from a specialist supplier. This could be purchased either packaged on a platform or as software to run on a platform that is already available (or obtained independently).

The creation of the full environment might be undertaken by the IS provider or by a specialist environment builder. Perhaps the most likely solution is for the IS provider to purchase a complete environment from an environment supplier, but to extend it over time with additional tools.

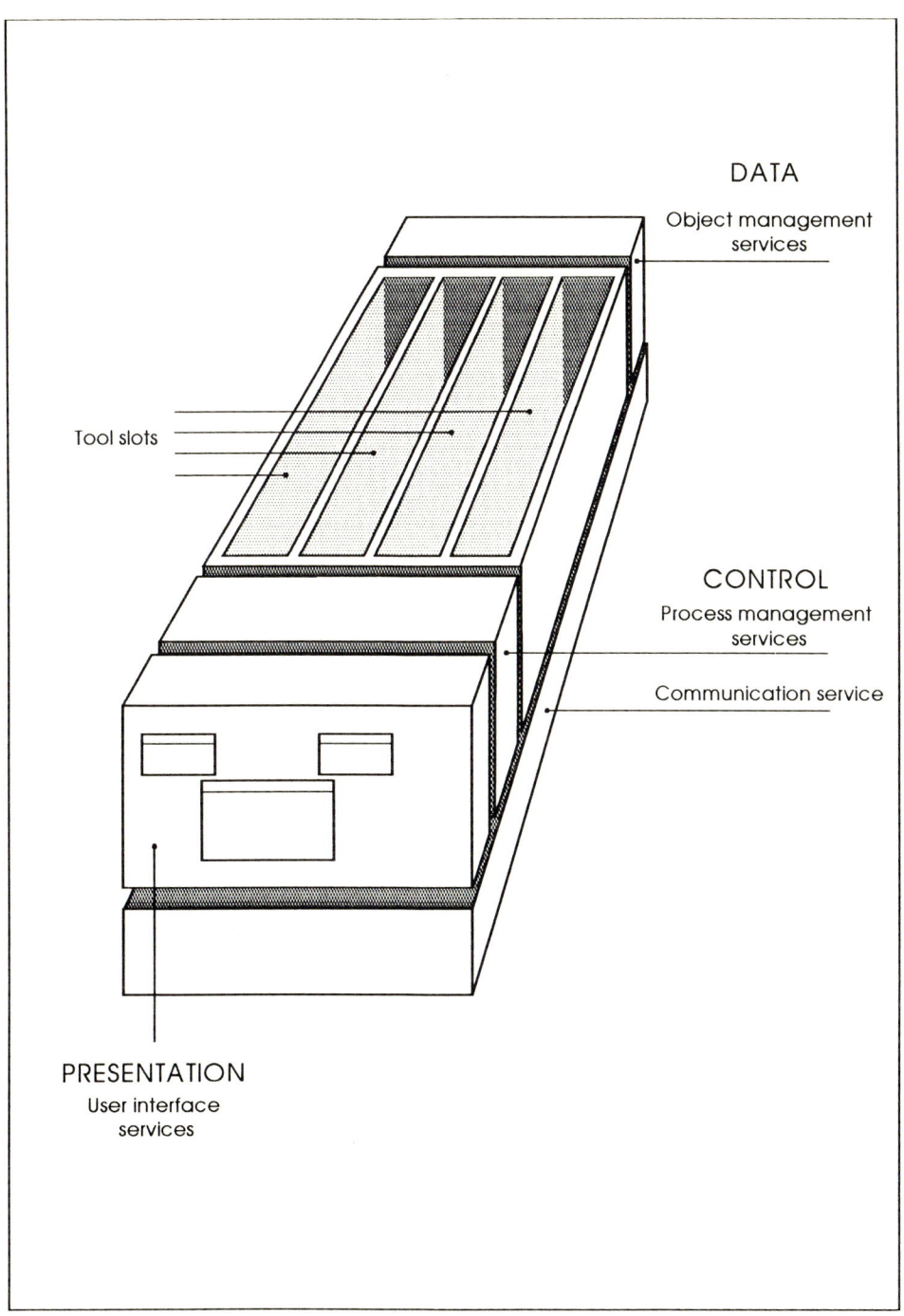

Figure 6: A pictorial view of the framework reference model

It can be seen that the existence of multiple suppliers is implicit in this idea of environment building. An environment from one supplier may be built on a framework from another supplier and a platform from a hardware manufacturer. The tools it contains may come from different suppliers, or may be written specifically to meet the requirements of the IS provider or customer. These same tools can be used in more than one environment, and may run on more than one framework, if they have been written using portable languages and PTI.

4 The PCTE standard

This chapter describes the PCTE standard and how it helps meet the requirements set out in Chapter 3. It is intended to give the reader a clear understanding of the issues that the standard seeks to address, its acceptance and likely evolution, and its relationship to other standards.

4.1 What the PCTE standard addresses

PCTE is a de jure standard for a set of public tool interfaces and an open repository which addresses the needs of producing an open systems engineering environment. It does this by providing access to a set of facilities which create an infrastructure for tools that support systems engineering projects. These facilities are independent of the machines and the operating systems on which they may be made available.

The PCTE standard defines a PTI providing data and control facilities which are outlined below. These facilities will be common to any systems engineering environment conforming to PCTE, whether it comes from one supplier or is built up from a combination of sources.

Data storage and management

PCTE provides a set of facilities to allow the storage of data in a common repository (known in PCTE as the *object base*) and to ensure that it is manipulated in a consistent way. These include version management facilities that can be used to control the coherent development of items in the object base.

PCTE defines how data should be represented in the object base. It gives detailed data models (schemas) for four central areas (system information, accounting, security and the data modelling metamodel). No other specific data models are prescribed, since environment requirements will vary considerably, but PCTE gives a consistent way of defining data models for the storage and use of information specific to each environment.

Chapter 5 gives more information about the facilities of the PCTE repository, and Annex A about data modelling concepts.

Running programs

PCTE provides a set of facilities to run programs (which might be both tools and software under development). These include facilities to control the running of programs on *foreign systems*, such as another development environment or a target system running a different operating system. Facilities are also provided to support the monitoring and debugging of software being developed.

Passing information between programs

Because all data is kept in a single repository, and is modelled according to a consistent set of rules within the environment, different tools can be designed to access the same data. This means that any program can use information that has resulted from the operation of another program. For example, timesheets completed by programmers could be used by a project management tool to monitor the progress of the project and by accounts staff to calculate salaries. In addition to this, there are also facilities for passing information between programs while they are running. Messages can be passed between tools, and can be generated automatically to provide notification of particular events.

Auditing and accounting

The auditing facilities allow the automatic recording of data access operations. The accounting facilities allow the automatic recording of the consumption of environment resources.

Data protection and security

Facilities are provided to protect data against errors,exceptions and failures. These facilities, which are described in Chapter 5, cover the consistency and reliability of data, prevention of unauthorised access to information (including disclosure, amendment or deletion of information) as well as resilience in the case of system failure.

Chapter 4
The PCTE standard

Distributed processing and data storage	The PCTE preferred structural architecture is a network of single-user workstations and the associated resources. Facilities are provided to handle distribution, so that users working in such a network need not be aware of where data is stored or on which machine their program runs.

4.2 Areas that the PCTE standard does not address

User interface	The PCTE standard makes no attempt to define a specification for a user interface. Instead, it recommends the use of an appropriate de facto user interface standard such as the X-Window System X-Library standard, which is well established throughout the software industry and available for a very wide range of hardware.
Common data models	The PCTE standard does not prescribe data models beyond the essentials of any systems engineering environment. However, many of the organisations and individuals who have been involved in the development of PCTE are also involved in current initiatives to develop common data models. These will define data types for the most frequently required data areas, such as software development in particular programming languages. The public availability of such models will encourage tool suppliers to model data in a way which makes the best use of PCTE and will improve the openness of environments, as discussed in Chapter 6.
Communication between environments	PCTE does not define facilities for communication of information between PCTE environments or between a PCTE environment and another system. However, this area is the subject of an ISO standards initiative (Software Engineering Data Definition and Interchange, or SEDDI) which brings together the Technical Committees responsible for ECMA PCTE and EIA CDIF (see section 4.7).

4.3 Evolution of the PCTE standard

The first version of PCTE as a formal standard was issued by the European Computer Manufacturers Association (ECMA) in 1990 and 1991. It is expected that PCTE will shortly be submitted for consideration as an ISO standard.

The PCTE standard is the result of a lengthy period of cooperation and consultation between interested parties from the computer industry, the defence industry, government departments and academic institutions. This means that the standard has taken account of practical needs found during the development of prototype environments, as well as theoretical requirements identified, for example, by the work on reference models and the US CAIS initiative.

The development of PCTE began in 1983 as ESPRIT project 32, which produced an early version of the interface specifications (PCTE 1.4). This project addressed the requirement for portable tool interfaces in the context of distributed hardware, a shared database and graphical user interfaces, while seeking to maintain compatibility with Unix System V. These specifications were later revised and implemented, as PCTE 1.5, to take account of X-Window System, which was emerging as the de facto standard in this area.

From 1986, development of PCTE continued in a defence context within the PCTE+ project. This was a collaborative European programme, in which the UK played a leading role, which addressed both military and civil requirements. Standardisation work began in 1988 building on PCTE+ and the earlier versions of PCTE. Developments during this period included the addition of security and accounting facilities, which were not covered in earlier versions, and changes to make the standard independent of particular programming languages or operating systems. Conversely, the specification of user interface facilities, included in the remit of the original ESPRIT project, was removed and replaced with the endorsement of a de facto standard during this period.

Chapter 4
The PCTE standard

4.4 Form of the PCTE standard

The PCTE standard consists of three volumes:

- The abstract specification (ECMA 149) which describes the concepts and operations in a language-independent manner. This volume is a good source of technical detail about the concepts, as it contains comments and annotations giving a rationale for the scope and structure of PCTE. It consists of a number of clauses, each covering a specific topic (for example, data management, security, accounting). Each clause defines a set of data types and operations relevant to the topic

- C language specifications (ECMA 158) for the operations, for inclusion in tool source code written in C

- Ada language specifications (ECMA 162) for the operations, for inclusion in tool source code written in Ada.

The C and Ada specifications are known as 'bindings'.

4.5 Commercial and government acceptance

Because the PCTE standard has been developed on the basis of implementations and evaluations of earlier versions of the interfaces, commitment to the standard is high amongst both vendors and user organisations.

Although at the time of writing at the beginning of 1993 there are no full commercial implementations of the ECMA standard interfaces, a number of suppliers are already developing commercial implementations of the ECMA standard interfaces, which are expected to be released around the end of the year. A commercial implementation of the PCTE 1.5 interfaces has been available since 1990, which has been used as a framework for a number of environments.

The aerospace industry, with its requirements for authority, stability and reliability, has endorsed the use of PCTE, in particular with respect to traceability of data and long-term support. PCTE is thought to provide a good basis for the creation of customised development environments needed in this area, by reducing framework and tool building effort.

In France, an environment based on PCTE has been developed for the French defence ministry for its own use and for use by its suppliers. In the United States, PCTE has been selected in the context of a number of government contracts.

4.6 Conformance with the PCTE standard

Implementations of PCTE must comply with one of two conformance levels. At the higher level, implementations must conform with the whole standard. At the lower level, they must conform to the whole standard with the exception of certain of the security measures. Other than this there are no subsets of PCTE. These strict conformance requirements increase the portability of software developed in a PCTE environment.

At present there is no certification system but one is due to be developed as part of the European Community Conformance Testing Services programme, and another under the North American PCTE Initiative (NAPI) launched in 1992.

4.7 PCTE and other standards

An important consideration in deciding whether to commit to a particular standard is its compatibility with other standards that may be already in use in an organisation. The rest of this chapter examines a number of standards (both de jure and de facto) that are in common use and assesses their relationships with PCTE.

Chapter 4
The PCTE standard

Data handling standards

The US Electronic Industries Association CDIF (CASE Data Interchange Format) supports the exchange of software engineering data between tools and between CASE environments. CDIF and PCTE have many aspects in common, and joint initiatives are taking place to ensure they do not conflict.

An IRDS (Information Resource Dictionary System), supported by a limited family of ISO standards, is an information system that stores, maintains, controls and protects information within an organisation's information systems development environment. The information within the system is managed in a way that enables it to be shared and reused by CASE tools and by direct users. A number of standards are required to completely specify an IRDS. Two ISO IRDS standards currently exist. The first standard, known as the IRDS Framework (ISO/IEC IS 10027: 1990), specifies the overall architecture for an IRDS. The second standard is known as the IRDS Service Interface Standard (ISO/IEC IS 10728: 1993 and BS 10728: 1993). This standard specifies a service interface that gives any program (or CASE tool) full access to IRDS services. There is no compatibility between the ISO IRDS and ECMA PCTE standards and it could be argued that both ISO IRDS and ECMA PCTE are competing standards. This argument is countered by comparing the different repository standards to COBOL and FORTRAN — both are standards but they address different problems. The differences between the IRDS and PCTE standards are further explained in the Report published by Ovum — *Repositories and Frameworks: a Detailed Product Evaluation*.

SQL (Structured Query Language) is a widely used commercial query language conforming to IS 9075:1992. PCTE does not define a query language, although individual environments and tools may define and use their own query management system.

SEDDI (Software Engineering and Data Definition and Interchange) is the work of an ISO working group aiming to provide a standard interchange mechanism for the transfer of data that is commonly used in software or systems engineering. This work brings together the technical committees of EIA CDIF, ECMA PCTE and ISO IRDS.

Programming language standards

There are two different aspects of the relationship between PCTE and programming language standards. The first is the existence of standard language bindings. Each binding, which relates to a specific programming language, maps abstract PCTE functions to the functions which will be called within tools written in that language. The second is the relationship between PCTE and the programming languages that may be used to develop information systems within an application development environment.

- Bindings. The PCTE standard defines bindings for C and Ada (see section 4.4). A C++ binding is currently planned, although there is no C++ standard at present

- Development languages. PCTE makes no assumptions about the programming languages within an environment. Current environments include tools to support programming in C, C++, Ada and FORTRAN; COBOL support is likely to follow.

Platform standards

POSIX standards support the portability of applications software by providing a set of ISO operating system interface standards. POSIX has several features in common with PCTE (for example, process management and file contents management). Implementations of the PCTE standard running on POSIX compliant platforms are currently under development.

Chapter 4
The PCTE standard

Process and methods standards

PCTE makes no assumptions about systems development processes or the use of any particular methods or tools. Several of the existing PCTE environments support the enforcement of preferred methods by modelling the development process according to particular standards. Projects can then be set up automatically to contain the appropriate events, milestones and products at each stage.

CCTA does not recommend any specific lifecycle model, but there is no reason why a PCTE environment should not be used to model and support an organisation's IS development process in a similar way. For UK government organisations such an environment would probably contain the following, which are the UK Government recommended methods, unless some different specialised requirements have been identified.

- PRINCE (PRojects IN Controlled Environments) is the recommended UK Government project management method

- SSADM (Structured Systems Analysis and Design Method) is the recommended UK Government standard system analysis and design method for the development of IT based information systems, and thus relates to the earlier parts of the project lifecycle.

User interface standards

As described above, the PCTE standard recommends the use of an appropriate standard such as X-Library as the user interface portability platform for PCTE tools.

A graphical user interface toolkit such as Motif, which is built on X-Library and provides user interface components such as windows, menus, and message boxes, helps to define an integrated style of user interaction, and is entirely compatible with the PCTE standard.

Procurement standards UK GOSIP (Government Open Systems Interconnection Profile) defines the recommended selection of ISO OSI standards for the mainstream of government applications. Procurers of PCTE based application development environments should ensure that the environment also conforms to UK GOSIP specifications.

5 The PCTE open repository

The concepts of the PCTE repository or object base are central to the way PCTE supports open integrated development environments. This chapter introduces some of the main concepts, and shows their relevance to the development and maintenance of information systems.

Within an application development environment based on PCTE, the repository is a single, shared, database, which may be distributed over a number of storage devices on a network. The repository is accessible (subject to the necessary controls) to all the users and tools of the environment.

The repository holds or represents everything of interest to the development projects in the environment. This includes details of projects and personnel, the documents and software products they are working on, and the tools they use. It also includes all the data needed to control and administer the environment. During the course of systems development, the repository thus comes to hold a great deal of information, which represents a significant investment to both the IS provider and the IS customer.

Users and tools work with appropriate subsets or views of the repository, containing just those types of information that are relevant to the task in hand. This reduces the complexity of the visible data, and contributes to security.

5.1 The structure of the repository

The repository is structured as a network of *objects* connected by *links*. The objects are or represent identifiable data items such as tasks, people, programs or documents. The links represent the relationships between them, such as the author relationship between a person and a document, or the composition of a program from a number of modules.

The pattern of links can represent conventional tree structures as found in a file-and-directory based system, and objects can be used like files as 'containers' to store, for example, text or code. More interestingly, the network of objects can represent the much more subtle and complex relationships between data items as typically represented in databases. Objects do not have to represent file-sized items; a network of objects may be used to store a finer grained structure of data items and their inter-relationships.

An example showing the structure of the repository is illustrated in Figure 7. Here a requirements analysis task (part of a tree of tasks in the work breakdown structure of a project) has been allocated to Jan Jones of the Analysis team. The input to the task was an Objectives document, and on completion of the task (using appropriate tools) the resulting Catalogue of requirements was also stored in the repository.

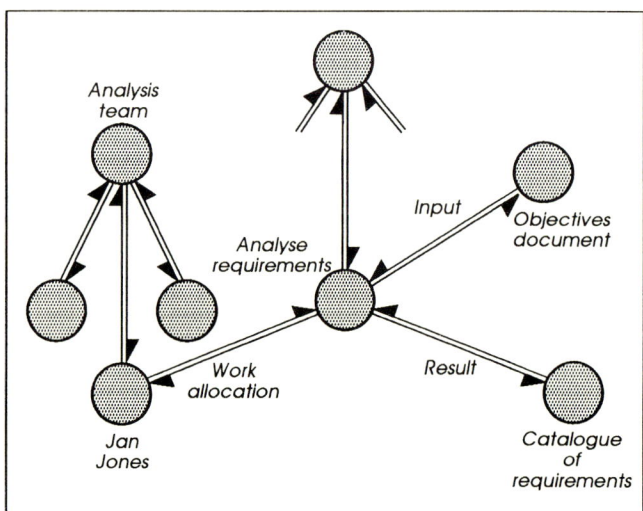

Figure 7: An example of data in a PCTE repository

Chapter 5
The PCTE open repository

Both objects and links can have *attributes*, recording more information about them. For example, the names of the members of the Analysis team and their grades might be attributes of the objects representing them. Attributes on links can be used as keys to name the links and to access objects.

Some objects, but not all, have *contents*. Contents are larger blocks of data which can be read and written like conventional files. An example could be the Catalogue of requirements in Figure 7, which might have been written using a word processor. The extent to which contents are used to contain structured data relates to the granularity issue discussed in section 5.1.1.

This repository structure gives a very direct representation of the data in the application development environment. It allows data to be accessed from its relation to other data. As far as is practical, items of interest are held once only. This reduces unwanted redundancy and inconsistencies in systems development information. For instance, the representations of program modules handled by a design tool can be physically the same objects as the files of source code created by the development teams and read by the compiler. Each tool and user has its own view of the relevant attributes and links to other objects. For example, the development teams might be interested in the test status and the coder responsible for a module, while the compiler needs links to the libraries to be used during compilation.

Composite objects

Many of the objects held in a repository represent items which are made up of a number of component parts. A simple example would be a program made up of a number of modules, or a book made up of a number of chapters. In larger projects, the concept of a *configuration* is important. For example, a delivered product may consist of a number of executable programs, some run-time parameter files, documentation and so on, all of which need to be gathered together and treated as a whole for issue and maintenance.

PCTE recognises these requirements in the definition of *composite objects*. A composite object is a tree of individual objects defined by a hierarchical link structure. Component objects can be shared by different composite objects. Operations can treat the composite as a whole, or allow processing of individual components. For example, a single operation could be used to copy a whole book from one project to another, or one of its chapters could be copied individually.

5.1.1 Granularity in the repository

Because there is a minimum storage requirement for each PCTE object, the PCTE repository is generally said to be suitable for coarse and medium grained data. Some tools handle data with a very fine grained structure, such as source code syntax. Because of the overheads involved, this type of structured data would normally be held within object contents, rather than being represented directly by objects, links and attributes.

It can be seen that there may be a trade-off between the efficiency of how data is stored and its shareability. The data modelling facilities of PCTE, discussed in section 5.2 below, allow tools to make their data models public and thus provide strong support for the sharing of data between tools. The sharing of structured data that is held in object contents, on the other hand, is not managed by PCTE data models. Research is currently going on to bring together work on fine grained data modelling and PCTE.

5.1.2 Versions

Many kinds of data kept in a repository change over time and must be held in more than one version. This includes programs, documents, project plans and so on. PCTE supports the versioning of objects, including composite objects.

Version operations allow multiple versions, and their histories, to be maintained. Depending on the requirements of a particular environment or type of data, access to versions can be controlled so that the latest version is selected automatically (in document editing, for instance) or a specific version is selected (to test a specific product version, for instance).

5.2 Data models

Data models in PCTE are handled by the use of data types and schemas to define models for particular purposes. The data modelling facilities in PCTE are very important in allowing environments to be extended and customised to meet the needs of particular systems development processes and tools, in enabling tools to share data, and in making sure that users and tools can work with appropriate views of the repository.

It should be noted that the data modelling facilities of PCTE are entirely concerned with modelling tool data and with the organisation of items of interest within the applications development environment. They are not concerned with modelling data for the information system under development, which would be handled by appropriate tools, depending on the target database system and the chosen system design methods. IS developers using a PCTE environment do not therefore have to undertake any PCTE data modelling activities. They will, however, make use of the data models of the environment in accessing data in the repository.

Annex A defines some of the data modelling terms that will be met in literature about PCTE, and explains how the data modelling concepts affect the nature of PCTE environments.

5.3 Data protection and security

The tools, products and other data held in a repository are very valuable assets, and their accessibility and reliability are of vital importance to the production of information systems on time and to specification. PCTE provides a number of facilities to protect data against errors, failures and exception conditions.

Consistency   If a data operation involves a number of stages, a
                       failure part way through the operation could leave
                       inconsistencies between the data items that have been
                       updated and those that have not. For example, if a
                       project schedule was being updated, it would be
                       important that all the tasks were updated consistently.
                       If the update failed, then the entire schedule should be
                       left unaltered.

                       PCTE allows tools to address this requirement in two
                       ways. If the tool has its own error recovery
                       mechanisms, updates can be applied immediately, and
                       the tool can perform any 'cleaning up' needed in the
                       event of a failure. Alternatively, the tool can make use
                       of PCTE *transactions*, which provide a roll-back facility.
                       In this case, the updates made during the transaction
                       are only applied if the transaction is successfully
                       completed. Otherwise the repository is returned to its
                       state at the start of the transaction.

                       Transactions can be nested. This is important for tool
                       cooperation, where tools can call other tools. Each tool
                       can use transactions to meet its own requirements,
                       without taking any account of transactions that might
                       be used in another tool. Only when the outermost
                       transaction is complete will changes be committed to
                       the repository. The PCTE transaction facility also allows
                       some actions to be explicitly excluded from the
                       roll-back in the case of failure. This allows error
                       messages and diagnostic information written during the
                       transaction to be preserved.

                       Transactions are a special type of PCTE *activity*.
                       Activities are also used to lock data so that only one
                       tool can access it at a time. This is also important in
                       ensuring consistency, since it prevents the problems
                       that can occur if an operation is based on the value of a
                       data item when it starts, but the data value has been
                       changed by the time the update is applied. Locking is
                       done at the level of individual objects and their
                       associated links and attributes, not at the level of
                       physical pages as in some traditional databases. This
                       prevents unnecessary loss of access to large parts of the
                       repository.

Privacy   There is a need to protect against unauthorised access to information, and against accidental or malicious damage that could be caused in this way.

PCTE provides two mechanisms to cater for privacy requirements. The first is *discretionary access control*. These facilities are always available, and allow access to be controlled according to the user's identity or the group he or she works in. The second, *mandatory confidentiality* is intended for highly secure systems and may not be implemented in all environments. It is based on defined sets of security classifications (for example, 'confidential', 'top secret'). Users are only allowed to read objects with the same or a lesser confidentiality level as their own, and are prevented from writing classified information to a less highly classified object.

Integrity   In any environment, not all tools and users are equally reliable. The confidence that can be put in data will vary according to its source. It may be important to be able to classify this level of confidence, taking into account the ability of a user to amass information, or of a tool to process information. In particular, data considered to be highly reliable must not be made less so by unreliable users or tools, or by the use of other data in which there is less confidence. This requirement is of particular significance to quality management during the development of safety-critical systems.

Integrity can be safeguarded to some extent by the use of discretionary access control as described above. For more complicated requirements, PCTE provides *mandatory integrity* facilities. These operate in a similar way to mandatory confidentiality, by classifying data, users and tools.

Resilience | Where data is distributed over a network, it is important that a failure of one part of that network does not prevent the use of the repository altogether. If there is a network failure, or a failure of one of the data storage devices, it should be possible to work locally at a workstation that is still functioning. This is addressed in PCTE by maintaining replicated copies on every workstation of all the objects declared as being system-critical. The existence of these copies means that it remains possible to run PCTE, even though some or all or the non-replicated objects held on remote storage devices are inaccessible.

6 PCTE environments and tools

As discussed in Chapters 2 and 3, the use of an open integrated environment to develop information systems could offer dramatic benefits to the organisation or business that requires these systems. By using such an environment as a way of implementing and enforcing project management control, as well as expediting system development tasks, organisations may control costs, shorten the timescales and exploit useful information involved with systems provision. This in turn should lead to systems that are delivered quickly, are flexible and offer good value for money.

There is a growing body of manufacturers and suppliers that see PCTE as an essential feature of application development environments, and that are actively developing frameworks, environments and add-on tools that comply with the standard.

The fact that an environment is based on PCTE does not of course completely determine its nature. The standard is intended to be general enough to allow specialised environments to be built to satisfy the needs of particular application areas. It follows that different PCTE environments, from different environment suppliers, may have different features and may be more or less suited to a particular organisation's needs.

This chapter explains what a PCTE environment is, and the key considerations in assessing how well any particular environment meets the requirements and provides the benefits set out in Chapter 3. It defines what is meant by a PCTE tool, and how both PCTE tools and other tools can be integrated into a PCTE environment.

6.1 What is a PCTE environment?

A PCTE environment is an environment built on an implementation of the PCTE interfaces and repository. The way it is built up follows the approach described in section 3.5, as summarised below.

Platform   The platform consists of proprietary hardware together with a host operating system and/or a DBMS. PCTE may be implemented on any type of system, but the standard suggests a preference for a set of powerful, single-user workstations and associated resources communicating over a network. This is known as a PCTE *installation*, and a user working from one of the workstations has access to the total resources of the installation, subject to the necessary access controls.

The workstations and servers making up a single installation do not necessarily all have to be of the same type or come from the same manufacturer. Each processor will be running its own PCTE implementation. The network can also support (as foreign systems) machines which do not run PCTE . This allows the target systems for which software is being developed to be connected to the network, and for software to be down loaded and run from the PCTE workstations.

Repository   The PCTE repository may be implemented over the file system or database of the underlying platform. Current initiatives are also exploring the possibility of using object-oriented databases. The repository is generally distributed over all the available storage devices of the network. As discussed in Chapter 5, it contains not only all the data associated with the systems development process and used by tools, but also the data types and schemas that provide the data models of the environment.

The repository completely takes the place of a conventional file system or database, and is essential to full data integration. Nevertheless, a PCTE environment can make it possible to continue to use data held in the underlying system, or other systems on the network, by allowing tools that run on those systems to be incorporated into the environment. This is discussed further in section 6.3.2.

Chapter 6
PCTE environments and tools

Tool interfaces and common services

The PTI layer in a PCTE environment consists of the implementation of the PCTE interfaces as defined in the standard, complemented with a set of tool interfaces to handle the user interface (UI). Together these tool interfaces form a complete platform-independent layer, such that tools can be written with no knowledge of, or dependency on, the platform.

The framework may include further layers of tool interfaces or common services to simplify tool building (by factoring out common functions) or to increase integration within the environment. This may affect the openness of the environment and the portability of tools which use these services, as discussed below.

Tools

The tools of the environment, whether provided as part of the framework or added to it after initial installation, can be classified as 'PCTE tools' and 'non-PCTE tools'. PCTE tools are those which require only the defined PCTE and UI interfaces, and make no use of other interfaces that may be available on the underlying platform. PCTE tools may use the PCTE and UI interfaces directly, or indirectly by using higher level libraries, or by invoking other tools, which themselves use the standard interfaces.

PCTE environments may allow tools not written for PCTE but able to run on one of the systems on the network to be incorporated into the environment. This is discussed further in section 6.3.2 below.

6.1.2 Availability of PCTE environments

At the time of writing, a number of environments have been created, based on versions of PCTE that are effectively subsets of the current standard. Many of these environments have been built as part of research and evaluation initiatives, but several are either already available as commercial products or will soon be launched as such. These environments are available on a range of platforms.

6.2 Services provided by PCTE environments

An important consideration in deciding whether to specify a particular application development environment within a policy for IS provision is how well the services it provides cover the requirements of the systems development process.

The PCTE standard does not determine what services will be provided within an environment based on it. However, as outlined in Chapters 4 and 5, the interfaces and repository defined by the standard do provide good support for the development of the types of tools and services needed. For example:

- Data management in the repository is specifically addressed, including the data protection and resilience requirements of a distributed database, and data modelling of repository data

- Version management is specifically addressed

- The development of configuration management services, according to specific needs, is supported by composite objects

- There is specific support for connections to target systems and for running programs on them

- Many aspects of system administration (for instance, device handling, users, accounting) are specifically addressed. The repository is designed to contain data relating to system administration as well as data relating to development projects. This provides good support for system administration services, even where these necessarily relate to the particular implementation and platform.

The services available in any particular environment will include not only those provided directly by the framework or environment supplier but also tools from independent suppliers. The availability of services therefore depends to some extent on the ease with which tools can be obtained and incorporated into the environment. This is discussed further in section 6.3 below.

6.3 Openness of PCTE environments

As discussed in Chapter 3, the openness of an environment depends on three factors: the degree of hardware independence, the ability to incorporate tools from independent suppliers, and the reusability of data.

The type and degree of openness needed in an application development environment may vary depending on how information systems have been developed in the past and how they will be developed in the future. The type and degree of openness provided by specific environments may similarly vary. This section describes how PCTE environments in general address each factor, and the role that conformance to the PCTE standard has to play.

6.3.1 Hardware independence

As a set of Public Tool Interfaces defined by an international standard, PCTE strongly supports openness. During its development, PCTE has been implemented on a number of platforms, including POSIX compliant platforms, giving a wide choice of hardware.

The availability of a specific framework or environment on any particular platform depends on the policy of the supplier, but the environment will generally cover the widest possible range of hardware, in both homogeneous (same hardware) and heterogeneous (mixed hardware) networks. However, if some services of the environment have made use of any underlying properties of the platform, then these services may not be identical in all versions of the environment. For example, if the environment includes encapsulated non-PCTE tools, as discussed below, then these tools may not be available on all platforms.

6.3.2 Tool portability and availability

The portability of a tool is the ease with which it can be made available on a number of different platforms or within a number of different environments. The development of the PCTE interfaces was specifically aimed at the need to make tool code more portable.

PCTE tools using only PCTE and X-Library tool interfaces are inherently portable to all PCTE implementations of these interfaces. All that is required to make the tool available on the platform is to recompile the source code with the appropriate libraries. Tools which make use of higher level services built on the PCTE PTI (for example, common services of the framework, or the Motif toolkit) are portable to all environments containing these services. Since the services should themselves be portable, they should be available on a wide range of platforms, but they may not be available in all environments.

Although PCTE environments are open to the inclusion of PCTE tools from any supplier, at present most of the tools purpose-written for PCTE are cross lifecycle tools produced by environment and framework suppliers themselves. However, the level of take-up of PCTE, and the tool building support provided in PCTE frameworks and environments, should encourage new PCTE tools to be produced by a wide range of suppliers. This new generation of PCTE tools will fulfil the potential of PCTE as the basis for truly open environments, allowing method-specific tools to be selected at will and 'slotted into' the development environment.

Of perhaps more immediate concern is the use of existing tools within a PCTE environment. This is particularly important where there is already a commitment to certain methods and tools in the systems development process. Such tools can be made available in PCTE environments by either the tool writer or the environment builder.

Chapter 6
PCTE environments and tools

Porting existing tools to PCTE

Tool writers can make their tools available on PCTE by porting the tool code. This may be done simplistically, maintaining existing file structures and so on (rehosting the tool), or by making more use of PCTE facilities (re-engineering the tool). In the latter case, there would be changes to the tool's design, data model and source code.

Different tool suppliers have different policies about porting their tools. Some tool suppliers have a strong commitment to making the same versions of tools available as far as possible on all suitable platforms. Others see this as less important than continual upgrade of a product on a limited range of platforms. However, many established CASE market leaders have expressed a commitment to porting their tools to PCTE.

Encapsulating existing tools

Environment and framework suppliers may provide facilities to 'encapsulate' non-PCTE tools written to run on the underlying platform (or on other systems connected to the network). In these cases, services in the environment (*capsules*) 'wrap up' the non-PCTE tool and interface it to the rest of the environment. For example, a debugging tool written to handle C source code contained in a Unix file could be encapsulated so that it could be invoked from PCTE workstations in a similar way to other tools in the environment, and would operate on C source code contained in an object in the repository. The capsule would similarly handle the tool's output, so the user could access the results of running the tool.

The advantage of encapsulation is that it is not dependent on access to the tool's source code or on any form of porting by the tool supplier. The tool is simply used as issued for the chosen hardware. This mechanism has made it possible for existing PCTE frameworks and environments to offer a wide range of well established tools, and to be relatively open to the inclusion of other tools as required. In the case of upgrading to a PCTE environment without changing platform, encapsulation can allow continued use of existing copies of tools, and the data that they handle.

The disadvantage is that it may not be possible to integrate the tool as completely, nor take as full an advantage of framework services, as would be possible with a re-engineered tool. The portability of the encapsulated tool is not affected by the encapsulation, and so the tool will only be available on those platforms it has already been ported to, and for which encapsulating services can be provided.

6.3.3 Data reusability

As described in Chapter 5, and detailed in Annex A, all the data in the PCTE repository is defined by data models in terms of PCTE types and schemas. These are completely independent of any underlying file structure or database. Tools in the environment each have their own schema, and these are integrated so that they share data types. Data produced by one tool can thus be reused by any other tool that is integrated into the environment. Provided the tools themselves have a similar 'view of the world', it is therefore theoretically possible to replace, for instance, one design tool with another without losing the design data. It can be seen that the degree of openness that can be achieved in this respect depends on the level to which the data models can be integrated and standardised, which is further discussed in section 6.4 below.

The repository itself, or parts of it, can be transferred between PCTE environments provided the types and schemas are also transferred (or already exist in the new environment). The PCTE standard does not specify the mechanism to support such communication, but it does include a data modelling language which allows definitions to be transferred and types and schemas to be recreated or reintegrated in the new environment. This means products and project data created in one PCTE environment could be reused in another PCTE environment if required.

The transfer of data between tools (in the same or in different environments) that use different data models is not addressed by PCTE. This is however addressed by the CDIF standard which is discussed briefly in Chapter 4. CDIF will also be of importance in allowing data to be brought in from, and reused in, non-PCTE environments.

The requirement to import and export data can also be handled by services in the PCTE environment. Using techniques similar to the encapsulation of tools described above, PCTE environments can offer facilities to import data already held in an underlying or connected file system or database, and to export data from the repository to such a system. These facilities might be offered simply at a file level — to bring a document held in a file into a PCTE document type object, for instance — or they could provide more powerful and specific translation facilities to recreate a complete data structure held in a file or database using objects and links in the repository.

6.4 Integration in PCTE environments

PCTE provides many features that support integration.The level of integration within a specific environment, and the effect this has on the openness of the environment, depend on the policies of the environment builder and the design of tools. The following sections discuss some of the issues involved with respect to the three axes of integration defined in Chapter 3.

Data integration

PCTE defines an open repository which supports a very high level of data integration in an environment. In order for tools to share data within an environment, the tools' data models must be integrated so that they share any data types that they have in common.

The integration of a particular tool into a particular environment is performed by the environment builder or local repository administrator. It involves mapping the types of the tool's data model or schema onto equivalent types that already exist in the environment.

The ease and success with which this can be done with tools from different sources depends on the tools' data models, and in particular their agreement over the meaning and structure of shareable data.

The issues involved in designing a tool's data model are specialised and complex, and do not directly concern the tool procurer or tool user. However, it is important to understand that the design should have identified those types of data which could reasonably be considered 'public' and shareable, and that these should have been modelled using the repository in a way which is consistent with the likely integration requirements. Modelling 'public' data such as people, tasks, resources, product structures and so on within the contents of files, rather than as typed objects, links and attributes, is not prevented by PCTE, but clearly goes against its spirit and will reduce the shareability, and increase the redundancy, of such data.

In the long term, this requirement must be addressed by generally agreed standards for common data models. Work currently going on in this area takes account of the kinds of data models found most useful in existing PCTE environments, including the types defined within the PCTE standard.

Control integration

PCTE provides a number of features that support control integration. Tools can call other tools and tool components from within the tool code. Tools can also exchange data dynamically using message queues and notification mechanisms.

However, PCTE does not define how such mechanisms should be used, nor the format of messages. Particular frameworks may offer higher level functions such as message broadcasting. The degree of tool integration that will be achieved therefore depends to some extent on the policies of the framework or environment builder, or on agreement between tools. In practice, therefore, the closest cooperation will be achieved between tools that have been explicitly designed to work together, or to follow the same conventions as defined by a particular environment.

Specific environments may also provide support for the integration of tools within a defined process. This facility can be used to define which tools can or must be used during specific tasks of the process.

Presentation integration

Since PCTE does not provide presentation interfaces, the only level of presentation integration that it implies directly is that achieved by using the recommended X-Library interfaces. These may provide some 'cut and paste' facilities between tools so that, for example, text can be transferred from one editor to another, or screen dumps incorporated in documents. However, the use of these interfaces does not determine the common 'look and feel' of an environment, which will be the concern of individual environment builders.

Both graphic and dialogue aspects of presentation integration are addressed by facilities and conventions in specific frameworks. PCTE frameworks often include toolkits such as Motif, which provides user interface components such as windows, menus, and message boxes. Tools using these libraries can be tailored to some extent to conform with the preferred graphic style of the environment or its users. Environment suppliers may seek a higher level of presentation integration by supplying style guides to tool builders and by providing other support services to promote an integrated dialogue style. For example, the environment may define a preferred format for screen messages, or offer a service to handle message text for tools. Tools which comply with these formats, or use these services, are then better integrated into the environment than those that do not.

Although not explicitly addressing presentation integration, various aspects of the PCTE repository can be used to support it. The fact that data models are explicitly held in the repository makes it easy to associate particular icons with particular types of data, ensuring that the user always recognises data on the screen. Similarly, data types can be associated with tools or functions, making it possible to provide an integrated object-oriented user interface. The user can be offered a menu of appropriate operations on data of a particular type, rather than launching specific tools.

The typing of data also makes it possible for tools in an integrated environment to offer more meaningful cut and paste operations. For example, pasting the icon representing a user into a structure representing a team can be interpreted as allocating the user to the team, while pasting the same icon into a document might insert the full name of the user as author.

7 Choosing a PCTE based development environment

This chapter draws on material elsewhere in this volume to summarise the issues that should be considered when choosing a development environment that is based on the PCTE standard. The chapter starts by outlining the aims of IS provision policies, and the circumstances in which the use of an application development environment may be desirable. The next two sections of the chapter outline the relevance of PCTE to the choice and construction of application development environments, and the procurement considerations for PCTE-based products. The chapter concludes by providing checklists of the potential benefits and costs of making PCTE part of the policy for IS provision.

7.1 Aims of defining IS provision policies

Policies for ISE define how the organisation is to specify and obtain the ISE services it requires. By defining how its information systems development services are to be provided, an organisation can avoid proprietary lock-in and can gain control over essential features of those systems — their quality, timeliness, cost, and the ease with which they can be modified or reused.

7.2 When an application development environment is appropriate

Application development environments offer support for, and control of IS development. However, they also impose costs and responsibilities. This section summarises the factors that should be considered when deciding whether the use of an application development environment is relevant to the organisation's IS provision.

The benefits to be gained from using an environment are listed in section 3.2. Generally, a computer supported application development environment offers greatest benefit when the information systems required are complex or safety critical or when the development team is large or split amongst different IS providers. Development environments may also be necessary when the development process needs to be formally recorded, for example to facilitate future maintenance.

The use of an application development environment presupposes that IS development takes place within one or more clearly defined lifecycles and that appropriate methods are used for design, debugging, change management and so on. If the way the organisation develops or procures information systems does not follow this premise, then the benefits of using an application development environment will not be gained without some change of organisation and procedures. In this case, it would be difficult for the IS provision policy to specify in advance the details of the environment and tools that should be used.

7.3 The role of PCTE

Where the use of an application development environment is appropriate, the environment chosen should be both open and integrated. It should be possible to build the environment up from hardware and software from a number of different sources, to provide the tools and services that are needed for the organisation's IS development. The environment should contain an open repository, allowing tools developed by suppliers to share data.

PCTE supports these objectives because:

- PCTE is a public, de jure standard. Conformance to PCTE does not conflict with conformance with standards covering other aspects of environment building and integration, notably GOSIP, POSIX, de facto user interface standards and CDIF

- PCTE defines an open repository and strongly supports data sharing among software tools

- PCTE defines a set of portable tool interfaces which strongly support platform independence and integration between tools from different sources

- PCTE is supported by hardware manufacturers, tool builders and framework and environment suppliers, indicating that there will be an increasing choice of PCTE products and suppliers. There is vendor commitment to the concept of multi-supplier environment building, including the encapsulation of non-PCTE tools where required.

At the time of writing, the market does not offer a wide range of commercial implementations of the full PCTE standard interfaces nor a variety of environments and tools from a choice of suppliers. Conformance to the standard could not therefore be specified as an immediate requirement in an organisation's IS provision policies. However, PCTE environments and tools built on earlier versions of PCTE, with a clear upgrade path to the current ECMA PCTE standard, do exist and PCTE environments based on the ECMA standards should be more readily available during 1993 and beyond. Where PCTE is considered to be the right approach, a technical policy might reasonably specify that any application development environment should have a commitment to conforming to the standard, with full migration of existing tools and data. The policy might also specify that tools selected now should be capable of being run within such an environment in the future.

7.4 Procurement considerations

One of the main reasons for considering PCTE is that it is a standard supporting open systems which can therefore help the organisation to avoid proprietary lock-in to particular manufacturers, tool suppliers, environment suppliers, or IS providers. The policies for IS provision in general and ISE in particular need to be specified in such a way that the organisation retains flexibility of choice in all these areas, and the final choice of products and suppliers must take this into account.

Commitment to PCTE in a technical policy does not predetermine which CASE tools should be used. First and foremost, the tools must be suited to the lifecycle, methods and techniques that the organisation wishes to use. A PCTE based application development environment will be procured from a supplier and the need for and possibility of tool integration into that environment must be evaluated. Clearly, tools designed or re-engineered for PCTE potentially offer a much higher degree of integration than encapsulated or rehosted tools. However, the degree of integration of any particular tool into any particular environment will depend on the design of the tool and the environment.

Factors that affect the procurement choices for environments and tools are as follows:

- Provision of ISE services. Do the proposed environment and tools support the required ISE processes and methods?

- Openness. Can the proposed environment run on several platforms (and are these platforms ones the organisation is happy to use now and in the future)? Can the proposed tools be used in several environments? Is it possible to take information systems developed in one environment and continue their development or maintenance under another? Is it possible to import existing tools and data into the proposed environment?

Chapter 7
Choosing a PCTE based development environment

- Integration. How well integrated will the proposed tools be in the proposed environment? In particular, are the tools' data models designed for integration?

- Performance. How well do the proposed environment and tools perform on the proposed platforms?

- Costs and Benefits. What are the costs and benefits of purchasing an environment, or of including specification of environment in a call for tenders? What are the costs and benefits of using environments? (See section 7.5).

7.5 Costs and benefits

This final section lists the potential costs and benefits that may result from the use or specification of a PCTE environment for IS provision. The costs of using a PCTE environment are likely to fall on the provider of ISE services, whether this is the organisation itself, its contractors, or the creators of off-the-shelf products. Where the organisation is not providing its own ISE services, therefore, the costs may be reflected in the price of tenders or products under consideration. The benefits, on the other hand, include both direct benefits to the ISE service provider, and also the resulting benefits seen in the developed information systems.

Costs

- Hardware. In general, the use of a PCTE environment will require its own hardware, additional to hardware used for running the developed information systems. The ideal configuration is likely to be a network of workstations, which must include sufficient memory, disk storage and other resources to support the efficient use of the environment.

    The hardware costs implied by specifying the use of PCTE depend on the size of development project and on whether the ISE provider already uses one of the many platforms that will support a PCTE environment

- Software. The software costs are those for the PCTE framework or environment itself plus the add-on tools required. However, if the environment offers appropriate encapsulation facilities and the ISE provider already has tools that run on the underlying platform, it may not be necessary to repurchase tool licences

- Training. The use of a PCTE environment will require some investment in training, in various degrees, for ISE managers, development teams and system administrators

- Implementation. There may be costs associated with the project to implement a PCTE environment or to migrate to one.

Benefits

- Management and control. Because all project data is held in the repository, project managers have direct access to information about work in progress. The integration of tool data supports integrated project management and work flow systems, which gives a high level of control and facilitates quality assurance.

  The design of the repository supports the security, consistency and accuracy of designs, schedules and other project data in the repository

- Multi-vendor approach. The openness of PCTE gives the freedom to change environments and IS providers without loss of investment in tools and data. Platform, framework and tools may come from different suppliers, allowing choices to be made on the basis of requirements and value for money

Chapter 7
Choosing a PCTE based development environment

- Flexibility. A single PCTE-based environment may be used to develop IS for different target systems. Products of the software development process are held in the repository and are immediately available for maintenance and for reuse in other developments

- Ease of use. A PCTE-based environment can give system developers access to data and tools as and when they are needed, and can offer a common 'look and feel'. PCTE supports the integration of modular tools and sharing of common functions; this reduces duplication and improves the consistency of services

- Preservation of existing ISE investment. PCTE environments may incorporate existing hardware, tools and data.

Annex A: Data modelling in PCTE

This annex defines some of the data modelling terms that will be met in literature about PCTE, and explains how the concepts affect the nature of PCTE environments.

A1   Types

Each object, link and attribute in the repository has a type, and is said to be an *instance* of the type. Typing classifies data. For example, the repository might include object types 'document' and 'task', and an attribute type 'status'. Specific documents and tasks, represented by objects, would be instances of the document and task types respectively. Specific status attributes would be instances of the status type. The type defines certain properties that all instances of that type share. For example, status attributes might be limited to a range of values defined for the status attribute type.

In the case of object types, there is an additional feature known as *inheritance*. More specific types (specification documents, say) are defined as specialisations of more general types (documents, say). The specialised, or child type, inherits properties from its parent types and may add to these. This allows a graph of types to be constructed, with shared properties defined at the highest common level and automatically assumed at lower levels.

The inheritance feature is important in allowing objects to be recognised at an appropriate level of specialisation for a particular tool or task. It allows data to be shared with differing levels of detail of meaning. For example, it might be important to a project management tool to distinguish between specifications and other types of documents, while the document publication service called upon to print a specification might treat it simply as a document.

A2   Schemas

A schema is a collection of types and the relationships between them. A schema is a data model which determines what instances conform to that model.

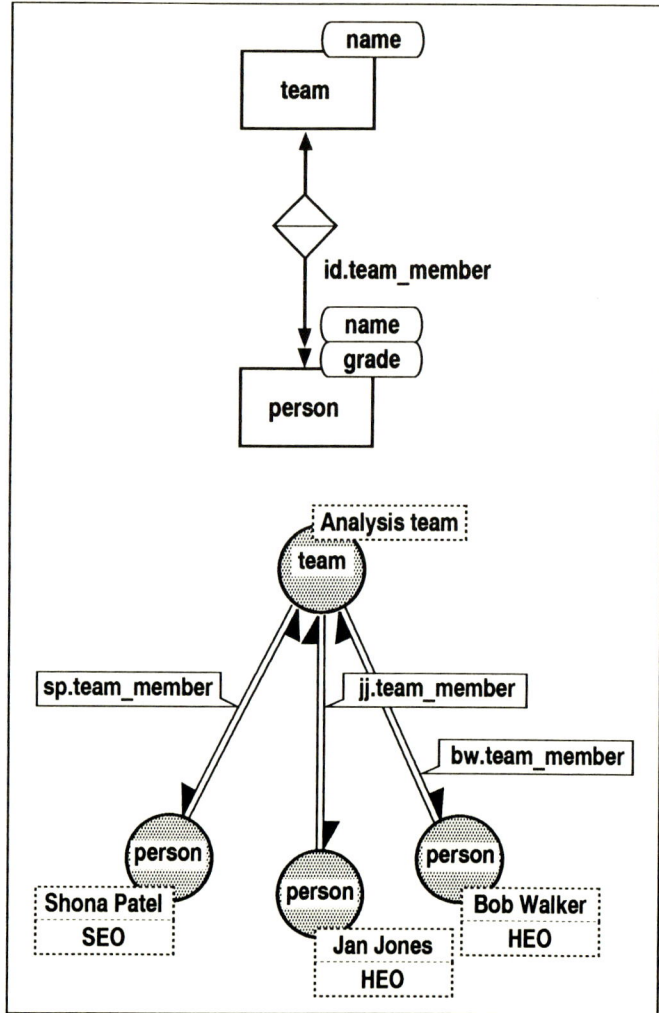

Figure 8: A PCTE schema and conforming instances

Figure 8 shows a very simple schema describing a team structure model. In this example, each person can only belong to one team (single arrow) but a team can be made up of a number of people (double arrow). People belonging to the team are identified by a short key. Full names and grades are recorded as attributes. An example of a possible set of instances in the repository, conforming to this schema, is also shown.

PCTE uses two sorts of schema. Firstly, data models are defined in a static way within the repository using Schema Definition Sets (SDSs). The PCTE standard includes some predefined SDSs which are used by the PCTE interface operations. Other SDSs are defined by tool designers, to model data as used by the tool, or by environment administrators, to organise data so that it can be accessed easily within a particular environment.

Secondly, the view of the repository seen at any time by a tool or user is defined by a working schema, which is composed dynamically from a selection of the stored SDSs. That is, it can be changed by users and tools as necessary to give the required view. These concepts are defined in more detail below.

Schema Definition Sets

SDSs are the basic mechanism used in PCTE to define data models. Each SDS is a collection of types and their *applications*. Link types can be applied to object types, and attribute types can be applied to object and link types. For example, in Figure 8, the attribute type 'grade' has been applied to the object type 'person'.

The same types can be included in different SDSs, with different applications if required. This allows tools to use independent data models which may nevertheless be integrated within a repository so that data is shared. New data models can be added at any time without affecting existing data and models.

For instance, in the example in Figure 8, the person object type might exist in a number of different SDSs, each dealing with different kinds of relationships or attributes. An SDS designed for document management, for example, might apply link types representing an authorship relationship between person and document, but might not include the grade attribute type.

Working schemas

The working schema is a mechanism for giving each tool (and associated user) a tailored view of the repository. It is composed from a list of SDSs. Only instances of those types defined in the SDSs will be visible to the tool; all other types will be filtered out and will thus be invisible. However, the inheritance mechanism described above means that objects of specialised types not included in the working schema will be seen if one of their parent types appears. In this case they will appear to be an instance of the parent type or types, and only those properties defined for the parent types will be visible.

The use of working schemas removes unnecessary complexity in the use of the repository, only presenting appropriate types for the tool in use. The working schema can be changed to allow different types to become visible, as necessary and allowed in the circumstances. The mechanism can be used to hide data in order to control the use of tools or actions of users. In this way it strengthens the privacy and integrity facilities, so that unauthorised users are not only prevented from accessing certain objects, links or attributes, they are not even aware of their presence.

Different working schemas effectively present different databases, without losing any underlying connections. The working schema mechanism thus allows a PCTE repository to offer all the benefits of a single, shared database, while avoiding the disadvantages associated with such a large and complex structure.

Annex A
Data modelling in PCTE

A3   The metabase

Because the repository is designed to hold all the data relevant to the environment, data models are held in the same way as other data. Types and SDSs are represented by objects, while the grouping of types in SDSs and the application of types are represented by links between these objects.

The part of the repository that holds this information is referred to as the *metabase*. The data model that describes its structure is called the *metaschema*.

The metabase is important because it makes the data models explicit and allows them to be accessed like other data in the repository. This means that within particular environments additional information can be associated with the data types. For example, the icon to be used to represent objects of a particular type on the screen can be linked to the type in the metabase.

Data models are also defined using Data Definition Language (DDL). DDL provides a common format for the understanding and exchange of schemas. PCTE includes facilities to build the appropriate metabase structure for an SDS described in DDL, and to create DDL from an existing structure.

Bibliography

ECMA documentation Free copies of the ECMA publications are available from:

ECMA Headquarters, 114 rue du Rhone CH-1204, Geneva, Switzerland.
Phone +41 22 735 3634
Fax +41 22 786 5231

PCTE Abstract Specification
Standard ECMA-149

PCTE C Programming Language Binding
Standard ECMA-158

PCTE Ada Programming Language Binding
Standard ECMA-162

Reference Model for Frameworks of Software Engineering Environments
Technical Report ECMA TR/55

GOSIP publications *Essential Guide to GOSIP* is available from the CCTA Library.

GOSIP version 4 Purchaser Set is available from HMSO
ISBN 0 11 330568.

ISE Library The ISE Library volumes are available from HMSO:

CASE and The Issues for Management
ISBN 0 11 330594 X

Database Language SQL Explained
ISBN 0 11 330583 4

Migrating from SSADM Version 3 to Version 4
ISBN 0 11 330576 1

POSIX The *Guide to POSIX* is available from the CCTA Library.

PRINCE documentation

The *PRINCE Reference Manuals* are published by NCC and available from the Publications Manager, National Computing Centre Ltd, Oxford Road, Manchester M1 7ED.
ISBN 1 85554 012 6

The *PRINCE Overview* booklet is available from the CCTA Library.

The following PRINCE guide is available from HMSO:

PRINCE in Small IT Projects
ISBN 0 11 330542 7

Quality management library

The Quality Management Library comprising:

Overview
QMS Implementation
QMS Audit
Quality Training
Quality Techniques

is available as a boxed set from HMSO.
ISBN 0 11 330569 9

SSADM documentation

The *SSADM Version 4 Reference Manual* is published by NCC and available from The Publications Manager, National Computing Centre Ltd, Oxford Road, Manchester M1 7ED.
ISBN 1 85554 004 5

An Introduction to SSADM can be obtained from the CCTA Library.

User interface Library:

A number of Guides are available from the CCTA

User Interface: The issues
User Interface: Style Guide Issues
User Interface: Style Migration Issues

Other publications	*Managing the Software Process* Watts Humphrey Addison Wesley 1989 ISBN 0 201 18095 2 *PCTE the standard for open repositories* Lois Wakeman and Jonathan Jowett for the PIMB Association Prentice Hall ISBN 0 13 065566 x *Repositories and Frameworks: a Detailed Product Evaluation* Ovum ISBN 0 903969 78 5
Addresses	CCTA Library, CCTA, Riverwalk House, 157-161 Millbank, London SW1P 4RT. Telephone: 071 217 3331 (GTN 217 3331) HMSO Publication Centre, PO Box 276, London SW8 5DT Telephone Orders 071 873 9090 Fax Orders 071 873 8200 General Enquiries 071 873 0011

PCTE - An Overview

Glossary

Activity	A framework in which a set of related operations take place.
Application development environment	A computer system supporting the development of applications.
Applications	Information systems or other software products developed to meet some external requirements, as opposed to system software or tools.
Attribute	A data item associated with an object or link in the object base.
CAIS	Common APSE Interface Set. A US initiative to define a PTI for Ada programming support. The requirements identified were taken into account during the evolution of the PCTE standard.
CASE	Computer Aided Systems Engineering. The use of specialised software or tools to support the production of applications.
CDIF	CASE Data Interchange Format, an Electronics Industry Association family of standards for the exchange/transfer of software engineering data between CASE tools.
Contents	Blocks of data associated with an object which can be read and written like conventional files.
CRAMM	CCTA Risk Analysis and Management Methodology.
DBMS	Database Management System
DoD	The US Department of Defense
ECMA	European Computer Manufacturers Association. A body producing standards and reports. Despite its name, it includes most major computer manufacturers in the world market.

Environment	An application development environment. Other terms with similar meaning are Systems (or Software) Engineering Environment (SEE) or Integrated Project Support Environment (IPSE).
ESPRIT	European Strategic Programme for Research and development in Information Technology. In this programme the CEC provided part funding for pre-competitive, cooperative research projects undertaken by consortia of organisations from the computer industry and non-commercial institutions within the EC.
Framework	The infrastructure of an environment, consisting of the PTI together with higher level services and a repository.
GOSIP	Government Open Systems Interconnection Profile (UK) recommends the selections and options from the OSI standards that are relevant to administrative computing.
Granularity	The fineness of data decomposition.
Integrated Environment	An environment in which tools work cooperatively, sharing data and providing a consistent user interface.
IPSE	See Environment.
IRDS	Information Resource Dictionary System supported by a limited number of ISO standards.
IS Customer	The organisation taking delivery of and using an information system.
ISE	Information Systems Engineering
ISO	International Standards Organisation
IS Provider	The organisation that develops an information system.
Link	A unidirectional association between two objects in the object base.
MOTIF	A windows oriented graphical user interface developed by the Open Software Foundation.

Glossary

NAPI	North American PCTE Initiative. A joint technical initiative amongst government, industry and academic institutions in North America. The initiative was launched in 1992 by the US DoD, NIST and the OMG (Object Management Group).
NIST	National Institute of Standards and Technology. This institute is a part of the US Department of Commerce.
Object	An identifiable item of data that needs to have relationships to other items in the object base.
Object base	The PCTE repository. A network of objects and links, qualified by attributes.
Open environment	An environment that can include hardware and software from a range of suppliers.
Open Look	A graphical user interface developed by Sun Microsystems and AT&T.
Platform	Hardware and related system software such as operating systems and DBMSs.
PCTE	Portable Common Tool Environment. A standard for a PTI and open repository. The acronym originates from the ESPRIT project 'Basis for a Portable Common Tool Environment' which produced the first version of the PCTE interface specifications.
PCTE environment	An environment incorporating an implementation of the PCTE interfaces and repository.
PCTE tool	A tool that uses only the PCTE interfaces, or higher level services built upon them, and makes no direct calls to the underlying operating system or DBMS.
POSIX	Portable Operating System Interface for Computer Environments — publicly available specification.
PTI	A set of Public Tool Interfaces. These allow tools to make calls for input, output and control that are independent of the underlying hardware or operating system.

Repository	A database in an integrated environment, holding software products and other data relating to software production and/or used by tools.
SEE	See Environment
SQL	Structured Query Language supported by an ISO standard.
Target system	The hardware and operating system on which an application is to run.
Technical policy	Technical policies form part of the IS Strategy. They provide the backbone of guidance and standards on the technical aspects of the strategy.
Tool	A program used to aid the production of other software. For example, a compiler or a change management tool.
Tool data model	A representation of the types of data used by a tool.
Type	In the context of PCTE, a template defining common basic properties shared by instances of the type in the object base.
UIMS	User Interface Management Service A service provided in a framework to handle tools' interaction with users.
Workstation	When used to describe a piece of physical equipment, the term implies a system that provides a single user with a powerful processor, providing a high quality user interface (high resolution screen, keyboard and mouse) and generally including its own disk storage. Workstations may be networked, and other systems on the network (servers) may provide further disk storage, processing power and so on.
	When used to describe a processor within a PCTE installation, the term implies a processor that is running PCTE, which includes both users' systems and servers on a network, or could be a single mainframe system.
XLIB	A functional interface to the windowing protocol of the X Window system developed at the Massachusetts Institute of Technology. It is regarded as a de facto standard.

Index

Abstract specification	33
Access control	45
Accounting	29
Activities	44
Ada	33, 36
Application	77
Development Environment	8, 15, 36, 77
Development Environment, when to use	59
Architecture	24
Attribute	41
type	67
Auditing	30
Axes of integration	22, 55
Back-end CASE	16
Benefits	14, 64
Bindings	33, 36
C	36
C++	36
CAIS	77
Capsule	53
CASE, Computer Aided Systems Engineering	6, 77
CDIF, CASE Data Interchange Format	31, 35, 36, 77
Change management	17
COBOL	36
Common APSE Interface Set	77
Common data models	56
Common services	25, 49
Communication between environments	31
Composite Objects	41, 50
Computer supported cooperative work	17
Confidence	45
Configurations	41
Configuration management	41, 50
Configuration management services	16, 50
Conformance	34
Consistency	44
Contents	41, 77
Contracted-out development	3
Control integration	23, 56

Costs	63
CRAMM	77
Cross lifecycle tools	6, 26
Cross-compilers	16
CSCW	17
Data	
Definition Language (DDL)	71
handling standards	35
integration	22, 55
management	29, 50
management services	17
modelling	17
models	29, 31, 43, 55
protection	30, 43
query services	17
reusability	54
DBMS	24, 77
DDL	71
De facto standards	19
De jure standards	19
Dialogue	57
Discretionary access control	45
Distributed	
architecture	25
database	25, 46, 50
data storage	31
processing	26
repository	25
Documentation management services	17
DoD	77
Down loading	16
ECMA	32, 36, 77
ECMA / NIST reference model	26
Electronic mail	17
Encapsulated tools	62
Encapsulation	53
Environment	13, 78
building	26
PCTE	47
ESPRIT	32, 78
Evolution of the PCTE standard	32
Execution	30

Flexibility	13
Foreign systems	30
FORTRAN	36
Framework	26, 78
Front-end CASE	16
GOSIP	38, 78
Granularity	42, 78
Group working	17
Hardware	24, 48
independence	51
Heterogeneous networks	51
Homogeneous networks	51
Horizontal tools	6
In-house development	3
Information Resource Dictionary System	35
Information Systems Engineering	4, 78
Inheritance	67
Instances	67
Integrated Project Support Environment	78
Integration	9, 21
axes	22
in PCTE environments	55
Integrity	45
International Standards	19, 31
International Standards Organisation (ISO)	31, 78
IPSE	78
IRDS	35
IS provision policies	3, 59
ISE	78
ISO	31, 78
Keys	41
Layered architecture	24
Libraries	20, 26, 57
Lifecycle	60
model(s)	5, 37
tools	6
Link type	69
Links	39, 78
Lock-in	9, 13, 59, 62
Locking	44

Look and feel	23, 57
Lower CASE	16
Mainframes	25
Mandatory confidentiality	45
Mandatory integrity	45
Message queues	56
Metabase	71
Metamodels	20
Metaschema	71
Methods	5, 60
Modular services	23
Minicomputers	25
Models	
lifecycle	5
process	5
Motif	37, 42, 78
NAPI	34, 79
National Institute of Standards and Technology (NIST)	79
Network	24, 31, 46, 48
NIST	79
Non-PCTE tools	49
North American PCTE Initiative (NAPI)	79
Notice boards	17
Notification	56
Object(s)	39, 79
base	39, 79
type	67
Object-oriented	
databases	42
user interfaces	57
Off-the-shelf systems	4
Open	
environments	79
integrated development environments	13
Look	79
repository	29, 39
Openness	9, 18
of PCTE environments	51
OSI	38

PCTE	79
1.4	32
1.5	32, 33
commercial and government acceptance of	33
environments	47, 79
environments, availability of	49
implementation	34
installation	48
open repository	39
project	32
scope of	9, 10
standard	29
tools	47
PCTE+	32
Performance	63
Platform	24, 48, 79
standards	36
Portability	52
POSIX	24, 36, 51, 79
Presentation integration	23, 57
PRINCE	37
Privacy	45
Procedures	17
Process	
integration	23
maturity	15
models	5
Procurement	
of ISE support	62
standards	38
Programming language standards	36
Project	
control services	17
management	17
PTI	20, 25, 29, 49, 79
Public	
data	22, 56
Tool Interfaces	20, 25, 29, 49, 79
Publishing services	17
Quality Management	14, 45
standards	5
Query management system	35

Re-engineering tools	53, 62
Reference models	15, 26
Rehosting tools	53, 62
Relationships	39
Replication	46
Repository	9, 25, 29, 39, 48, 80
implementation of	48
structure	39
Resilience	46
Reuse	54, 65
Roll-back	44
Running programs	30
Schema	29, 43, 68
definition sets (SDS)	69
SDS	69
Security	30, 43
SEDDI	31, 36
SEE	8, 78
Services	16, 17, 18
in PCTE environments	50
Software Engineering and Data Definition and Interchange (SEDDI)	31, 36
Software / Systems Engineering Environment	8, 78
Specification and design services	16
Specifications	16, 33
SQL	35, 80
SSADM	16, 37
Stand-alone systems	25
Standards	19, 29
need for	19
Style guide	23, 57
System administration	50
services	18
Systems development lifecycle	6
Systems Engineering Environment	8
Target systems	48, 80
Taxonomies	15
Technical policy	80
Toaster diagram	26

Tool	80
communication	30, 56
cooperation	23
data models	20, 80
interfaces	20, 25, 49
Tools	6, 7, 49, 80
in a PCTE environment	52
PCTE	47
Transactions	44
Transfer of data	55
Types	43, 67, 80
UIMS	23, 80
Upper CASE	16
User	
communication services	17
documentation	17
interface	23, 57
interface management services	23, 80
interface standards	37
Version	16, 42
management	29, 42, 50
management services	16
Vertical tools	6
Work flow	17, 23
Working schema	70
Workstation	24, 31, 48, 63, 80
X-Library	31, 37, 57, 80
X-Window system	31, 80